Parable of the
Good Samaritan

WRITTEN AND ILLUSTRATED BY
Helen Caswell

Abingdon Press
Nashville

PARABLE OF THE GOOD SAMARITAN

Copyright © 1992 by Abingdon Press

All Rights Reserved.

Library of Congress Cataloging-in-Publication Data

CASWELL, HELEN RAYBURN.
 Parable of the Good Samaritan / written and illustrated by Helen Caswell.
  p. cm.
 Summary: Retells Jesus' parable about the good Samaritan.
 ISBN 0-687-30023-1 (alk. paper)
 1. Good Samaritan (Parable)—Juvenile literature. [1. Good Samaritan (Parable) 2. Parables. 3. Bible stories—
N.T.] I. Title.
 BT378.G6C33   1991
 226.8'09505—dc20   91-36352
                                                                         AC

Printed in Hong Kong

Read Luke 10:29-37

The Bible says that we should love our neighbor as we love ourselves.

Once someone asked Jesus, "But who is my neighbor?"

To answer the question, Jesus told the story of the good Samaritan.

One day a man was walking along between the towns of Jerusalem and Jericho. It was a very scary place. The road went steeply downhill through wild, rocky country that everyone knew was full of robbers.

Suddenly, a band of these robbers attacked the man and beat him and stole everything he had, even his clothes.

Thinking they had killed him, the robbers rode
off into the wilderness. The man lay unconscious
at the side of the road, face down in the dust.
After a while his eyes opened, but he was too
badly hurt to get up, or even to cry out.

Then he saw a priest coming along the road toward him. The priest was from the church the man went to in Jerusalem.

"He will help me," the man thought.

But as the priest came closer, he crossed over to the other side of the road, and wouldn't even look at the man lying there. The man could hardly believe it, and he turned his head as far as he could to watch the priest walking away from him.

More time passed, and finally someone else came along the road. It turned out to be a Levite—a very important person in the church in Jerusalem. But the Levite crossed over to the other side of the road and walked right on past, pretending not to see him, just as the priest had. So the Levite disappeared down the road.

The injured man wept his tears into the dust. He knew that he would die if someone didn't help him soon.

As he lay there helpless, he heard the soft sound of hooves and the cheerful jingle of harnesses. He looked up and saw a man riding toward him on a donkey. As the rider came closer, the injured man could see, by the kind of clothing he wore, that he was a Samaritan.

Now, the injured man was Jewish, and the Jews and the Samaritans didn't even speak to each other, so the man thought that if the priest and the Levite hadn't stopped, the Samaritan certainly wouldn't stop either.

But, wonder of wonders! When the Samaritan saw the man lying beside the road, he pulled his donkey to a stop, got off, and knelt over the wounded man, shaking his head in sympathy.

Then from his saddlebags, the Samaritan took some cloth and jars of oil and wine. He poured oil and wine over the man's wounds to clean them and help them to heal, and he bound them up with the linen cloth.

Then, very carefully, the Samaritan lifted the man up and put him on the donkey. Walking along beside them, the Samaritan went along the road until they came to the town, and there they stopped at an inn.

The Samaritan got a room at the inn and made the injured man comfortable. He watched over him all night, and the next day, when he had to go on his way, he left money with the innkeeper to pay for the man to stay until he was well enough to travel.

Jesus told this story because he wanted us to understand that our neighbors are not just the people who live next door. When the Bible says that we should love our neighbors as we love ourselves, it means that we should love anyone who needs loving.

m.416